D1531962

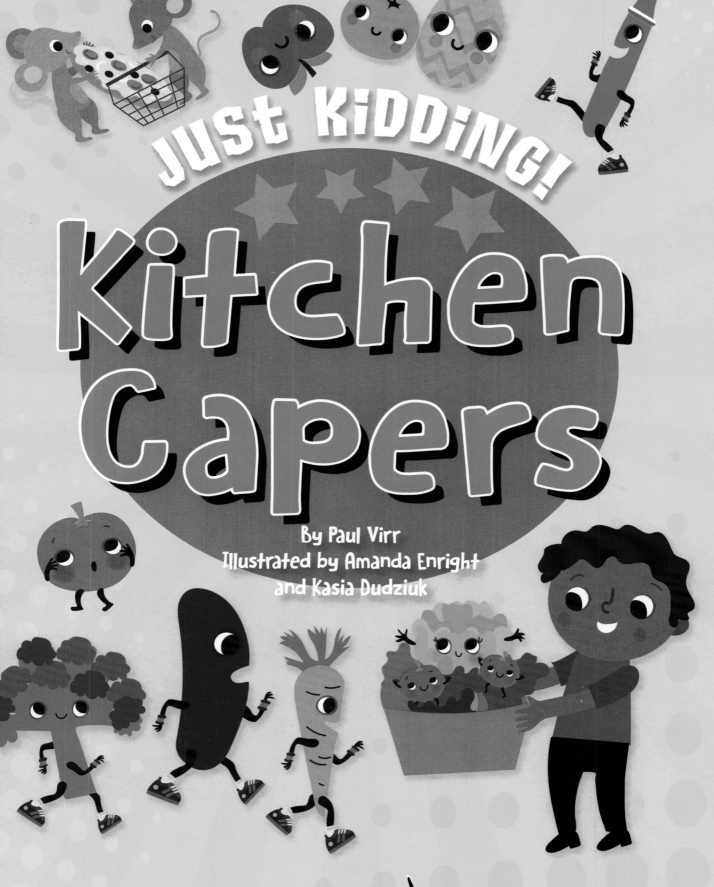

JUST KiDDiNG!

Kitchen Capers

By Paul Virr
Illustrated by Amanda Enright
and Kasia Dudziuk

WINDMILL
BOOKS

Published in 2020 by Windmill Books,
an Imprint of Rosen Publishing
29 East 21st Street, New York, NY 10010

Cataloging-in-Publication Data

Names: Virr, Paul.
Title: Kitchen capers / Paul Virr.
Description: New York : Windmill Books, 2020. | Series: Just kidding! | Includes glossary and index.
Identifiers: ISBN 9781508197935 (pbk.) | ISBN 9781538391228 (library bound) | ISBN 9781508197942 (6 pack)
Subjects: LCSH: Food--Juvenile humor. | Wit and humor, Juvenile. | Riddles, Juvenile.
Classification: LCC PN6231.F66 V577 2019 | DDC 818'.602--dc23

Manufactured in the United States of America

CPSIA Compliance Information: Batch BS19WM: For Further Information contact Rosen Publishing, New York, New York at 1-800-237-9932

Contents

Fast-Food Fun!

What do toads
like to drink?
Hot croak-o!

Did you hear the story
about the giant burger?
It was pretty hard
to swallow!

An Apple a Day?

8

A Pizza the Fun!

Waiter, do you think my pizza will be long?
No, I think it will be round!

Why did the student become a pizza chef?
He needed to make some dough!

Silly Space Food

Why don't astronauts eat right after they blast off? **They've just had a big launch!**

What do astronauts drink in space? **Gravi-tea!**

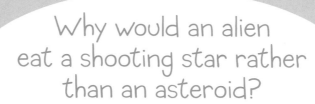

Dizzy Drinks!

What soft drink
do frogs like?
Croak-a-cola.

How does a
penguin drink juice?
Out of a beak-er!

Fruity Fun!

Soupy Loopy!

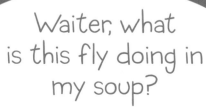

Silly Sandwiches!

A Fridge Full of Fun!

Why did the tomato turn red? **It saw the salad dressing!**

Why was the bean pod always running around? **He was full of beans!**

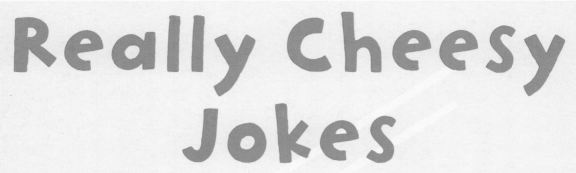

Glossary

apple turnover A dessert made from pastry filled with apple.

dough A mixture that is rolled out to make bread and pizzas.

fast food Food that can be prepared and served quickly.

meteor Small matter traveling in space at great speed.

satellite dishes Dishes that receive messages from satellites in space.

shooting star Another name for a meteor.

Index